ELIZABETH WILEY MA JD, POMO ELDER

Dragon Kites

Order this book online at www.trafford.com
or email orders@trafford.com

Most Trafford titles are also available at major online book retailers.

 www.trafford.com

North America & international
toll-free: 844 688 6899 (USA & Canada)
fax: 812 355 4082

Our mission is to efficiently provide the world's finest, most comprehensive book publishing service, enabling every author to experience success. To find out how to publish your book, your way, and have it available worldwide, visit us online at www.trafford.com

Because of the dynamic nature of the Internet, any web addresses or links contained in this book may have changed since publication and may no longer be valid. The views expressed in this work are solely those of the author and do not necessarily reflect the views of the publisher, and the publisher hereby disclaims any responsibility for them.

Any people depicted in stock imagery provided by Getty Images are models, and such images are being used for illustrative purposes only.
Certain stock imagery © Getty Images.

ISBN: 978-1-6987-0982-6 (sc)
978-1-6987-0981-9 (e)

Print information available on the last page.

Trafford rev. 11/15/2021

Dragon Kites

Stories of peace and joy on earth.

Oh God, our shelter from the storm, Give us Peace on Earth

1st Edition

Dedication:
To the WORLDS CHILDREN

This book is a special request.

We were asked, just ten days ago, to compound a book, one that will be translated into Spanish, Portuguese, and if we find the right translators, into Native Nation languages of the children, not just in America in child holding facilities, but the languages of children in refugee and orphan programs around the world.

Chapter One:

The reason children need help today, and have needed help for most of history…..help children build strength from their horror, do NOT help them build self-pity, anger, hate that will harm their young lives.

CHILDREN: no matter what culture we learn about, history has millions of children left alone, from war, disease, crime, natural disasters, parents starving from famine.

THE NATIVE AMERICANS had their children rounded up by bounty hunters and soldiers, dragged to Government Schools where they were punished for speaking their own languages. The favored method in the 1700 and 1800 and early 1900's was to heat a fire place poker to red hot, and burn the tongues of any child or teen that was overheard speaking their own language.

Most of these children never saw their own families again. Often the boys were drafted and sent as support or expendable (meaning missions in which they were not expected to return) troops. The girls were often "trained" as teachers, but were in fact a disrespected kind of teacher's aide in rural schools, they were given a place to live, often in a barn of someone in the community, and that was that. Nothing further was expected, or hoped for. Other young women were sent, on the weeks they were supposed to go back to their home lands and family, to be unpaid trainees, or low level nursing aids in homes of the rich. Again, they got housing, often in an attic corner, or basement room but were not allowed to go to town, or even to church. When they finished "school" they were simply given away to hospitals around the country that needed low level nurse aids and women to clean the rooms for women patients.

During and After the Civil War, women and girls, often without anywhere else to go after the men and boys in their family were killed in the war, would be minimally trained, and spent to help in field hospitals with the few doctors available. This included women of all races, and cultures, and many once wealthy women and girls who no men to support them after losing all male members of the family to the war.

World War I and World War II were not much better, often children of men killed in the war had no one, except mothers who were broken, and had to find housework or sex work to support their children. While during the war, when shortage of men the women had worked in many positions, after the troops came home, the women were expected to take off their shoes, get pregnant and stay in the kitchen again until the next war demanded their services while the men were marched off to war.

After World War I and World War II many orphan children from war zones were sent as refugees to America and other countries. The famous movie about the ship called Exodus, almost completely filled with children and teens, no one knew where most of them came from, were accepted into the desert of Palestine, and given desert to build small farms and ranches, known as Kibutzim to learn to live and survive. They were NOT all Jewish children.

The point of reporting all this horror is to help children, often who do not know why the world was so scary and horrible their parents tried to find a dream in another country. Often who did not, and do not know who their parents are. DNA does give a chance for them to learn what countries they came from, BUT, not always.

Help children? How does this help children? It helps all children in these horrors today to realize that it is not the first time in history, probably won't be the last, and they are not the ONLY ones. AND many have survived and been happy, learned to live happily ever after.

Another fact we want to pass along is that all Americans are NOT rich and harming others. Many Americans are so poor they are fed by food banks, or they will starve. Others are fed by food stamps. Others can barely afford food paying for the taxes and rising costs of food due to so much of the food supply being donated to food bank resources. Many Americans, thousands, maybe millions, have nowhere to live, or they live in cars, old campers, and garages, or tents under the freeway overpasses.

WE, all of us alive on this earth, have to take a part in resolving these problems. Once and for all.

I heard an inspiring story some years ago, a young girl, just turned 18, and released from foster care, with no known family, and nowhere to go, had done well in high school, had dreams, and started college. As she faced a dismal, alone holiday, she advertised for a family for the holidays. The news media picked up the story. She found a really nice family of people who gave her a place to belong. While we all know reality is that lonely, alone kids often are taken advantage of and harmed, there ARE great, wonderful families that will open up and let in another heart to love them and share their happy days, and their support when it is hard.....

One of the most heartfelt desires of this book, and the classes for children around the world who NEED support and love, is to help them know what love and support look like, and to go out and find it. And to avoid the kind of mean people who prey on others who are lonely and/or afraid. God bless our children, and elders who also find themselves needing support and love in a lonely part of their lives.

Chapter Two

Dragon Kites:

A story that can get YOU thinking, doing, enjoying.

Summer Day Reflection Song: Donovan

Music is a big part of my life. This song, in part says "Dragon kites in the sky, wheel and turn, spin and fly"……

One day I met the Grandfather of a child in a lunchtime Scouting program for immigrant children. His grandchildren had brought him to meet me, and tell us about the ancient Dragon kites that children played with in many Asian countries.

The families had problems with speaking in American, some of them came from countries that spoke English, but American had so many daily words that they did not know that they call it American.

They felt they needed help to put their children into growth programs that are generally run by parents of the children, so I volunteered to go at lunchtime to a different school twice month, and help many children join the Scouting they wanted and at the same time integrating all the parents together into a community of that school. The goal was to get parents, teachers, principals and aides to continue to run their own lunchtime Scouting programs. Every family could find at least one adult, or older teen to come one lunchtime a year and help with the meeting and inspire the children. This is much easier today as Scouting has online support and membership. An added benefit was that many of the parents, and grandparents had always wanted to be Scouts, but not been able to, so were able to enjoy and learn from the programs along with their children and grandchildren.

One of the Grandfathers, who took care of the children so the parents could all work, was asked by his grandchildren to help all the Scouts make Dragon Kites. I had heard of Dragon Kites in a song long before performed by Donovan in concerts

He gave us a list of things to bring in two weeks.
Every person showed up with many special things they had brought to decorate their Dragon Kite.

Dragons: and Dragon kites. Look online, find many dragons, and decide what YOUR kite is going to look like. There is even a paper dragon on a toothpick for a drink in some Asian bars that is perfect for seeing how you might shape your dragon from paper. Look for Dragon kites, and a history about them. I found dragon kite kits for as low was $10, and super crafted one of a kind dragon kites for $8500 plus shipping.

The Grandfather told us of his old days in Vietnam, once living on a farm, and his Grandfather making beautiful dragon kites out of the thin, wonderful newspapers he picked up when he walked the Grandchildren to the Mission school and as he waited for them. He would walk around and gather things that he kept in a special box of things to make Dragon kites. Sometimes he would do some work for a shop keeper and make a little money to buy some special ribbons, beads or decorative paper for the kites. Sometimes he would find decorative thin tissue paper used by shop keepers to wrap packages, and buy the sheets of tissue for a few pennies each.

Look online, find patterns, and kits for simple kites. Make some. Try to fly them. BE CAREFUL of telephone, electric, cable lines, and stay sat least a mile away from the huge satellite cell phone towers, and the even larger electric energy transport poles and lines. Way out on the desert, on a mountainside without many trees, and beaches are all good places to fly kites. A few parks are big enough, and without energy or cable poles and wires to safely fly a kite. BE SAFE. Also do not run over other people. BE AWARE.

There are busses in some of the big cities that go to the beach five days a week to minimize the beach traffic and parking problems during summer months. Call and find out if your metro transport system has this system. Get a cylinder packing box to roll up your kite and take it to a safe kite flying place. DO NOT GO alone, and always make sure it is OK with parents,.......THIS IS A WONDERFUL summer youth program field trip! Remember to take large trash sacks, and small bags so each person can pick up what they brought, and to pick up at least one more small grocery bag of litter to keep our public areas clean and safe! Look around your community and see if there are people who used to make kites, especially dragon kites, in their childhood or teens with the elders of their family. Look for seniors who made them, or still make them to get advice!!!!

Look up the different nations that fly, or used to fly, dragon kites. Some were for special occasions, or special meanings in their nation. Look up your own family history, did your family nation culture have any type of kites, or dragon kites for special occasions, or to celebrate beautiful breezy days? Kites are a beautiful and fun way to share something, no matter what the day, or the location you are sharing your kite.

Here are a few tips were learned from the Grandfather that was shared with our program by his Grandchildren: and by others we asked along the way as we looked for the paper, the wood, the design, and the memories of flying dragon kites from their old countries, or after they came to America to bring something special and awesome with them.

Materials: Get a small box, or bag to keep the materials you collect to make, or upgrade your kite each spring and summer when kite flying weather comes to your local area.

PAPER: Christmas and other holidays are great times to gather tissue paper of many strengths, and colors since they often are in packages. Try Asian stores, even the beautiful paper that often wraps fruit or toys can be ironed and used for parts of a dragon kite. (be careful when ironing, you don't want a fire!). Kids ask an adult before ironing paper.

ORNAMENTS, just about anything small and/or light weight enough is awesome. Today we have items not available in the old days. Glitter glue! Acrylic paint that dries fast, but lasts a long time. Kite wood as well as online teaching tools to learn how to make the kites from bamboo, and sticks. We discovered that the hollow lightweight stalks of our fennel plants when dried are a great resource if we can not find the lightweight bamboo. In the ancient days, small fibers of plants were often used as the strings to bind the dragon kites, today we have fishing stores and craft stores with large selections of strong, long lasting strings. In the old days, resin from plants was often used for glue, today we have many choices of glues.

In the old days, found feathers from wild birds, and feathers from farm chickens were plentiful. Today craft stores as well as fishing and hunting stores keep a large assortment of feathers for fly tying, and for creating arrow feathers tips. These all make wonderful additions to the kites.

Native American craft stores, online and at Native American art fairs and shows usually have booths that sell many kinds of feathers for use to decorate your dragon kite.

It is up to you to use the kite, or to hang it on the wall as artwork. You could take the kite to schools, and library talk days and show the children about these lovely and mythical links to the past of several Asian cultures. The Vikings had a long history of loving dragons on their flags, carved into their ships, their history is another great place to find an assortment of dragon pictures and stories from history.

Chapter Three

SKUNK HUNTIN'

This is a story from my childhood. The point is to ask young people to look into the lives of the older people they know, and find out all about things in their lives.

When I was a child, I lived in San Francisco in a beautiful bow fronted house on Geneva St. Then my Dad was released from the military hospital at the Presidio and we moved home to his Rez.

I truthfully do not think my "city mouse" Mom ever thought they would sell that beautiful home and buy a long silver trailer and move to the Rez while my Dad built his dream home there. City "mouse" would not be a great description of my Mom. She was super smart as a kid, and was moved up and up, and went to UCLA as a young teen. She got Masters in History and English, and a nursing education with cool little cap, and somewhere joined the Red Cross as an Army Nurse. She attended Berkeley as the "New Deal" programs began and got another Masters in psychology and social work, as well as her license for being a public social worker, in children and family services in San Francisco, Santa Barbara, and Los Angeles, along with teaching while she went to school at UCLA to pay for her university degrees.

By the time she met my Dad, she was a Phd student at Berkeley, working on her paper on what today is called PTSD. She was working with the Commander in charge of what was then called Battle Fatigue. She met my Dad while walking around a General and a movie star who were handing out medals.

He was a Native American from what was finally given recognition by President George W. Bush as an elite Native American paratroop unit of the Army. These were more generally known, along with the Black, Latino, Asian, and poor farm boys as the "expendables" dropped behind enemy lines to shoot until they were shot to keep the Nazi's from doubling back, or getting supply lines through prior to D-Day. As far my father knew, they did not even have medics, except for the training they were given to care for one another. They were told that no units would be available to come and get them until after D-Day and the expected routing of the Nazi air and ground forces.

My Dad was shot. Many others were dead, or dying and no care, or hope. My Dad relied on his Native American survival skills and set off through forests and did what he could to survive with only one leg. He would not know until he did find a US unit so long later that his army haircut had grown below his shoulders. The General who came to give him his medals commented that he had no idea such a great soldier would look like a little girl. My Dad was also not even twenty years old that day in that hospital.

The recruiters had said this was the "war to end war" and after the genocide of Native Americans, my Dad thought an end to war would be a grand event and wanted to be part of it. His Mother had escaped the bounty hunters who used dogs and horses, to round up the children on reservations to take them to BIA schools. She would run up the creek, and up the mountain climb a tall tree and hide. The dogs lost the scent from the water long before they found a tree and exposed her. She was illiterate. Signed her name with an X. My Dad told her to sign, so she did. He had lied about his age to get to go be part of "the end to war".

He was really 21 when I was born, they had to have dated at least a year, he had been searching for American units for four years. D-Day, plus four years….to age 21. My Dad must have been 15 when he went to war, to end war.

He told me that my Mom and her Commander were interested in his recovery, both still in surgery after surgery, often with grafts from other bones and body casts to help the injured right leg, and the bone of his other hip or thigh used for the grafts to try and save his leg.

In those days, Native Americans were very superstitious and culturally negative towards missing limbs. So, instead of a leg removal and prosthetic, he endured infections, and bone surgeries over forty years before he got not only diabetes, but also another infection and had to have the leg removed.

While in the hospital and supposedly in bed, my Dad would sneak out to the motor pool and learned as much as he could about all types of military vehicles and how to build and repair them. He also worked on his BA in business (Native Americans were very restricted, even though war heroes and with the "same" VA education benefits of white soldiers) and began a job as an accountant at a huge corporation.

My parents bought a lovely home, but was noted above, my Mom did not seem to realize he was heart bent on returning to the Rez, building a house, and ranch when he was released from the Army.

Many of my Dad's relatives had farms and small ranches that they bought with their veteran benefits. My Mom, having been a social worker on similar programs, and not liking the thought that all these war heroes were being ignored, helped them get their benefits. Many of my Dad's cousins were the first college graduates in the State from reserves.

When we went to visit the farms and ranches, the children were often given buckets, or old paint cans, washed out and with a coat hanger to make a handle, covered in an old rag, or washcloth. The children piled into the back of someone's pick up and were driven down by the creek, or river, and started picking berries.

Because these were ranches, or farms, people often were around, so bears were not a problem. BUT, other wild animals sometimes were.

It was not unusual for children to come rushing out of the berry patches with a mad raccoon chasing them. The raccoons either did not want us to take "their" berries, or were afraid we would bother their baby raccoons hidden in the trees and bushes gathering berries.

When the older cousins who drove the truck filled with kids got out of the truck, radio blaring, and shouted that it was time to go home, the kids all ran to the truck, more berries on their faces and clothes than in the buckets or pails, and laughing and eating out of the pails got back into the pickup truck for the ride up to the house or barn. The little old ladies had a pail of clean water, and some bowls and pans to divide the berries.

Some were put in bowls for the workers and elders to eat. Some were mixed with sugar and some spices, little pats of butter, and sprinkled with corn starch or flour and turned into pie shells they had prepared. Apples and any other fruit was added into the pies, or made into separate pies. All the paid workers, and the family members from their own homes, or ranches and farms had come to help with sheep shearing, fruit picking, or other end of summer chores to ready the ranch for fall and then winter.

One day, a truck load of kids went laughing and eating into the berry bushes by the creek, for awhile the sounds of laughter and fun were heard, then screams that brought the teens, jumping out of the truck, running. A stampede of little kids ran out, some with buckets, some without them, covered in juice and rushing to the truck and diving up into the truck bed.

Back by the berry bushes, lazily looking at the mob of screaming kids, picking at the dropped pails of berries was a family of skunks. The rest of our young years we referred to berry picking as "skunk hunting" and were a lot more cautious when entering the berry areas after that experience.

My Dad told us, YOU are the ones stealing their berries, and they will not hurt you, the only defense they have is to spray at your, but be careful not to get sprayed, it takes weeks in herb baths to get the smell off and you have to throw your clothes into the fire.

I still love skunks, but have great respect for them when they come into my stables in the dusk, or dawn to see what the horses have left for them. They rarely spray a horse, they are used to them, and know it is a great place to grab grain and other snacks that the horses have dribbled out of their mouths while eating.

Chapter Four

Seaweed

Seaweed, in Northern Coastal Native Nations was one of the best foods ever. The families got together and with cars and trucks packed to the breaking point went to gather seaweed, and abalone, and other sea foods, smoke them for winter use.

Huge bonfires were built, and everyone brought food to share for the day or two of gathering and drying seaweed.

The children would roam the beaches, the summer sea homes for our ancestors for what now has been documented to have been at least ten thousand years.

The children would find what we called "olive" shells, little snail like critters that star fish, and octopus as well as squid would put tiny holes in, and suck out the little snails. The empty shells would wash up with the tides. We gathered them for our Aunties and Grandmother and her sisters to use in art, baskets, and on clothing for special dance, or to sell. There were many types of tiny snail that had the pre-drilled holes in them from the animals that had caught and sucked them out. AND we found tiny abalone shells, also victims of some undersea animal dining on them. These were usually a beautiful pearly inside, often smaller than a dime. and sometimes with the familiar hole drilled by some sea creature to suck out the tiny abalones.

My Dad and other grown cousins would gather large drift wood, and the kids would gather smaller wood to use for the smoking and cooking of fish. Many of the family members brought store bought, or home ranch raised chickens, ducks, geese and pork or beef to roast for the big barbecue meals while the seaweed and fish were drying or smoking for storage.

In the old days, beautiful baskets held these foods, in our days, plastic pails, and store bought plastic containers, often sealed with brown paper bags were how the fish and seaweed were stored for winter use. The seaweed was dried, and often stored in big brown paper grocery sacks, kept just for that purpose.

On taking the items home, most did not wait for winter, but began to use the dried fish, and dried seaweed in meals. Many of us, like my family, had veterans who had spent time in San Francisco, or who had family members who drove to San Francisco to the huge jeans and tee shirt mills to work during the week. They shared overcrowded but fun small houses (more like shacks) while they worked to save money for homes, or for more education to help them help their families since there was little, if any, unclaimed land to live in our ancient ways during the fifties and sixties. Yet no matter where people were, they showed up for a day, or the whole week to gather sea weed, and dive for abalone and fished for fish to smoke. Often deer and elk were hunted on huge white owned ranches and farms where the animals had learned there were huge orchards of food, but the farmers and ranchers wanted them at least thinned as they often ate the whole crop, or the bark off the young trees, killing them.

Chapter Five

"Root" and baskets

"Root" when we were children on the rez, or visiting Aunties, or others with our Grandmother had several names in our own language.

My Mom worked, my Dad was often in the hospital, we were taken care of by relatives on and off the Rez (or I was in Pasadena with my Grandparents there if no one could care for me).

The most usual object called "root" was any type of bulb or roots that were eaten. We would walk with little baskets, or bags and gather them with the Aunties or Grandmothers we were accompanying to find "root". When my Dad was home, on leave from the Presidio Hospital in San Francisco, he would drive them where they wanted to go. No matter how many or what kind of casts he was sporting. He had crutches and could drive. Often he was actually supposedly at the hospital, he had just wandered off to visit his family.

The larger people sat on the seats of the car, or in chairs in the back of a pick-up, the lighter, and lighter on laps, the children on top. I liked those cartoons where the door of a car opened and a LOT of people poured out, that was our family going somewhere to do something with the Aunties and cousins and all the tiny kids.

The other type of "root" we would find and gather was an actual root of two different kinds of plants. Some were in marshy areas, and we would dig around, with big spoons for the kids, and sticks shaped a certain way as old ancestral tools had been. These roots were then washed, pulled into fibers, and dried. Some were dried with weights hanging on them to get them as straight as possible while drying. Others were just hung, or slung over a fence to dry and then sorted for certain kinds of basket work. As part of our Native environmental duty to Nature and to the next seven generations, we made sure we NEVER took ALL of anything. That the earth and marsh was patted back down for the growth to be healthy, and "root" to be available the next years. We did NOT dig where it was obvious from footprints and mud moved around someone else had recently dug.

One of the Great Aunties specialized in tiny baskets, she had one on display at the Southwestern Museum in Los Angeles for many years, before it was returned to a Northern California Pomo Museum. The tiny baskets were made of very fine root fibers, shredded to the size of threads, or just tiny strong grasses. The tiny olive and other shells, especially the red abalone (baby shells) were used to decorate these tiny baskets. Little feathers from chickens, grouse, ducks, and turkeys often were woven into the baskets with beads, and shells to decorate them. The basket at the Southwest Museum had tiny hummingbird feathers woven into it. The feathers would stick out the sides of the artwork of the tiny baskets.

Large baskets, made of the different types of "root" which included some willow fibers, were still used for various household chores, but most of the baskets by then, in the fifties were sold.

As time went on, more and more of the weavers began to use whatever they found to create their art baskets. Many kinds of beads, and beadwork as well as tiny gem stones, or beach stones that had been hand filed, sanded and rubbed with oils had holes drilled in them and they were also used in art baskets for sale. Many dyes began to be used by the artisan basket-makers. Shoe polish, coffee grounds, and a variety of fabric dyes produced what in the past had been unavailable to artists, or had not been produced yet by anyone. Today many weavers use commercially sold art dyes to get new types of colors for their art baskets.

When I was small, there were very finely woven baskets that were used to rinse and drain the acorn flour after grinding. Some of my Aunties put the acorns in a larger weave basket, set in a pan, and let it sit overnight. The acorns would be rinsed from time to time, the tannin water in the pan poured into a jar and left to dry in the sun. Some allowed these tannins to dry completely and stored the residue in small jars for a time when needed to condition hides from rabbits, deer, elk, moose or cattle. Even sheep or lamb skins could be finished in this tannin that worked when I tried it. The tannins created a soft, soft leather, with a silvery pearly sheen.

Many years later I was researching to find out what they had used, and found a book on many types of tannins and natural methods of treating hides for different feel, or color.

The book said to keep the outsides of acorns removed before grinding, and the water from rinsing the flour after grinding. It also suggested that burning oak logs, and saving the ashes, filtering them through fine woven baskets, would give a similar tannin to tan hides for the silvery soft leather.

Today many people simply buy commercial tanning compounds, or the leather already cured. I have never seen the fine, soft pearly leather except with the methods and tannins from the acorns and flour. I have found that by allowing the water to dry out and keeping just the powder, the hides cure as nicely as using tannin waters kept in jugs.

Chapter Six

REED BOATS

Every American has their own "reed boat" history. Whether Native Americans who survived escaping to deserts, the sea, or mountains, often only the women, taking the children, elders and disabled with them, or those who left every "thing" and came in a ship or plane, it took faith in a God we believe is only ONE, not the God of any religions, but the Creator of all, the entity beyond compression of us all, that existed from the beginning and will exist at the end of our little planet and the universe it travels in.

A Rabbi, who was also an AP Journalist, and a military security person sent in to Germany, behind lines, to find out what was going on in the secret facilities of the Nazis, because he spoke German, Hebrew, and American English. He said he found cities, where many people worked in what later became known as the concentration camps during the day hours, but did not talk, because they knew if they were caught even telling their wives, or fathers what they knew was going on in those facilities, from horrific medical experimentation on prisoners, to the "showers" in the death camps, their entire family, sisters, brothers, parents, aunts, uncles, and their own children and all the family children would be rounded up and put into the "work" camps. At that time the Germans could not be killed just for being Germans, as could the Jews, and some foreigners, but, as criminals against the Nazi State, they COULD be "terminated" or worked to death just as the others.

Dr. Victor Frankl, the famed survivor of the camps, in his books tells of not just the horrors, but the faith and hope, even after his own family was killed, or died that kept him going. One story that I kept in mind on any bad or sad day of my life was of when he had been sent to be a doctor in one of the camps. He saw his once boyhood home across the meadows and found, if he sat on the top of the sewage processing module (think of the stink of an outhouse multiplied many times) he could actually see areas he had loved as a young person. It gave him faith and hope to continue to help others and he then talks about the Nazi talking about the Americans coming, and taking the camp residents to meet them. He had a patient who was very, very ill, so said he would stay with that man. The guards did not want him to, but on reflection, he realized they did not want to make the other prisoners suspect their motives.

In reality, the Nazi soldiers took everyone else down the road and shot them, then buried the bodies, so the Americans could NOT find what had been there. More than likely they would have come back for him, but the Americans came and arrested or killed them in the gun battle. Sometimes God gives us miracles.

Chapter 7

Great-Aunt Olivia and the Telegraph in the Old West

People tend to think that money, position and comfort are all they need. Great-Aunt Olivia taught my Grandmother and her East Coast Daughters of the American Revolution friends otherwise. My Grandfather, taught men so wealthy their family still has streets named after them in New York and other big cities of the American Revolution, to find something else to do but to sit around comfortably in "the club" waiting for their older brothers and fathers to die, so they could take over the family corporations.

My Grandmother was allowed to go to college, of course one for women, and then her family put up with her eccentric dreams and let her go to law school. Being a lawyer, and being involved in the behind closed doors lives of other families, NO. And business, no way were they going to allow her to do something so guaranteed that no manly man would ever want her in marriage.

Her brother, a younger son, decided to go to medical school while waiting for his older brother and father to pass the corporations on to him…..he was a bit nervous, so my Grandmother went with him. BUT her parents surely did not see her poking around the bodies of strangers to be a doctor, so said NO. She became the Dean of the Rochester College for Women and helped other women reach her dreams.

Both my Grandmother and Grandfather decided to leave the social position, money and security behind and go out west.

Great-Aunt Olive had made that decision long before. She was a lady in New York society, and did NOT want to choose any of the eligible men who asked her. She did not want to reduce her life to telling the head housekeeper what she wanted, so the woman could get it done, while having tea with other women doing the same. Her big events of the year being family and charity "do"s.

She learned telegraph somewhere, and wrote letters from her "husband" and said he and his wife would like to come to a small wild west town and be the operators of the telegraph in the city they chose for them. She packed her bags, on them being accepted, went to a jeweler and bought a nice heavy duty wedding ring, suitable for a working man's wife, got on a train for the west, and started a new life.

When met at the stage station, she said her husband had been held in business for his family back east, and got on the stage and went to the city assigned to them. She said her husband had been detained, and rented a room in a proper boarding house. She started to work at the telegraph office.

Every time a stage came in she ran out to meet it, and acted sad when her husband was not on board. People began to be very nice to her, she did receive a short note from time to time saying he would be there soon. Then nothing.

She was so good at her job, she just remained, and spend her life in that wild west town. Over the years, she added dentures, and wigs, and tight corsets to keep her looking the same said my Grandmother. After some period of time she announced her husband had divorced her, and after some more time had passed she married a nice gentleman.

Great Aunt Olive had always worn a proper hat, and gloves to work, she hung the hat on a hat tree with her coat, but wore the gloves all day. The family did visit, the few who had courage to go and visit the old west in those times. My Mom said there were a few rude remarks made about the man she married, as much of an old maid as she. They had an outhouse, as did everyone in those days but had TWO toilet seats hanging on the walls, SHE was not going to put her behind on the same seat as a man!

Some asked, what a shock he must have had, when on their wedding night she took off her gloves, and wig, and took out her teeth….but they did have, as many couples did in those days, separate bedrooms, so maybe he never really saw her without all her attributes.

He passed away, she continued to send letters to her family, and to operate the telegraph station until her death. My Grandmother received a trunk and some boxes of her "things" after she passed, and what was left in her bank account after the sale of the home she and her husband had bought during their years together.

Chapter 8

Skiing on mud, crossing the Alaskan wilderness and high tea on the high seas (cruises with Grandmother and Great Aunt Lily)

My Mom, after her divorce, decided to go home and take care of her Great-Aunt Mable's mansion and estate, in exchange for taking my Grandmother and Mable on road trips, summer, winter break, and spring break…. One of the great breaks of having a family that has something to share, and wants to share it! Most divorced women with children did NOT have this opportunity, they got great jobs as housecleaners and taking care of bratty rich kids for tiny money. My Mom knew this, and had seen it in her work as a social worker, so SHE became the family for her clients, helping them get the education and skills to not just support their children, but to buy homes and start businesses to help OTHER single mothers. We were brought up on both sides of our family to thank GOD for the fact that no matter what losses and problems, we had a huge, loving, supportive family. It might not be the best dream to go live in the barn for four years at a relative's house while going to college, and learning skills to start a business. BUT, unlike most single mothers, our family had the barns, and the Aunties and Grandmothers to care for the children. On my Mom's side, she had a Great Aunt with a home she loved but could not care for any longer, and gave my Mom a place to raise the kids until they were old enough for her to go back to work full time.

This led to some exciting and strange experiences. My Mom got a new car of her choice every two or three years, and the use of it with insurance during the year if she also drove the two little old ladies to stores, and to doctor appointments. We all went to the same church, so church was included as well. Mable had been a Quaker, but rarely went to her Meeting Hall and if she did, she went with friends who picked her up.

AND……the agreement took in the holiday road trips. My Mother's Great-Aunt, being a Quaker, did not have the repressive attitudes towards women. She and her two sisters went to Cornell with their step-brother, and all became global botanists who went around the world finding plants, taking photos of them, of where they grew, and the people who grew them, and how they were used. Their catalog is today still one of the most complete ever prepared. They included water plants, algae and fungus in their studies, as well as ocean plants so were long ahead of most of their colleagues in ideas about environment, climate, and balance of nature. One of the sisters had passed, the other had married and moved to Bel Air and had a family, the brother had passed, and Mable broke her hip and decided to go live with my Grandmother in HER large empty house, and ask my Mom if she wanted to exchange the road trips, etc, for a great place to bring up kids. The house was named "Eisingwold". We on one side of the family lived on a Rez where there were no streets, and tiny though it was, no addresses, except for "the silver trailer down by the creek", or whatever. Many reserves today still have no street addresses and people live "in the old green van down past the three big rocks and the cactus". On the other in a mansion with a name, rather than an address.

Progress and developments had moved in, so "Eisingwold" ended up being 1085 New York Drive. The Rez is now a casino and parking structure with new land being annexed for a senior village, and a vineyard, and soon a leased land hotel. The Rez has a huge office in aa nearby town, and the address is on Airport Drive. Times change.

Mable wanted to go back, and see what once had been pristine lands as she and her brother and sisters had roamed, with little donkeys carrying their scientific equipment and tents before she passed. I think she was 83 when we started these road trips. We went to Alaska, she wanted to see the Glaciers, and the land before the planned PanAmerican Highway was built. So, dirt roads, and a lot of rain. It was not the season for snow yet. She taught us, as if she were teaching her college classes. We had no idea that other children did not learn geography and history while seeing the actual land, and old ghost towns, and abandoned mines. At one point there had been a "gold rush" and many people had come in big and small boats, that because they had no sense to find out the weather and terrain before leaving home, got stuck in the ice and snow. The people often perishing into the rapids of swollen rivers as the day was bright and sunny, but the floods from the melting ice came roaring past, tipping over the boats, and ships. There was no international rescue, there were no local rescues. People were just on their own. Many had no relatives who even knew they had gone out to Alaska, and they just perished, leaving nothing but rotting ships, boats, and mining or gold panning equipment behind in the mud and sand after the waters receded. Each year, for decades, the historical relics were buried in high flood waters, iced in, and then torn apart in the spring floods. We thought it was interesting to find bits and pieces of history and take them back to Mable in her chair, or the car, and find out what they "might" have been and how they ended up washed along the now dry beaches of the rivers and lakes of Alaska.

While the settlers, and miners brought genocide and fenced in and stole the lands of the native people, they have to be either admired for the faith in something better than the horrible, slum, rat filled cities they had left......or pitied as insane enough to set out, without proper knowledge of the weather, lands, natives, or the Russian and other fur traders and wood traders who had already taken large areas of the land as "theirs" simply killing off any natives who might suggest it was not their land and assets to take. Those vicious people defended the lands and assets they had stolen violently and relentlessly. A rough world.

The tiny museums, the ghost towns, and the history lessons on those road trips. We still had NO idea that all children were not growing up knowing and learning geography, history and botany as we were on these road trips.

The PanAmerican Highway was just being put in, many areas that had been one or two lane dirt, or gravel roads were being widened. The mountains along one side dynamited and shoved out of the way to form a four lane road. One spring, the ice was melting, and it was raining, without let up. The side of the mountain that had been dynamited was turning into muddy slurry and slushing into the rapidly rising river on the other side of the highway.

The road had fallen in completely at one point, and all the cars and a few busses were being taken out by small ferry. It was night, and four by four, the cars were ferried across the roaring river and left to find their way with police, and volunteer escorts down what was left of the small road on that side to safety. The busses, filled with passengers first of all had to turn around in larger areas of the road. Sometimes we saw the passengers standing in the icy rain while the bus driver backed and slid forward, backed again to get the bus turned around, and then, the busses began to go by, on the INSIDE side of what was left of the road. As often as possible the drivers were trying to find wider spaces so the bus did not push them so far into the slurry that their cars slid off what was left of the road, into the roaring, flooding river. The busses could only be taken one at a time on the small ferry, and they tore up the muddy, rain drenched roads. Many of the cars were becoming stuck in mud. Other drivers would get out and help, with shoveling the mud, putting rocks under the tires, and anything else they could do to help all the cars get to the ferry and across to safety.

WE had some great stories for "what I did on my vacation" when we got back to school.

Giant bear sightings. My Grandmother loved what she called "the dear berries", and would jump as fast as a seventy something woman could jump, out of the car and go off road when she demanded my Mother stop the car. We were quite sure she was going to eat poison berries and die. She didn't. Even Mable, who knew every plant warned her to at least wait until she took a look at the leaves and berries. My Grandmother just grabbed her berries and ate them. Until she sighted a bear family, and that was the end of berry picking for her.

One of these trips, again in spring, with rains, and flooding, the road trip planned went to Crater Lake in Oregon, and we learned about the volcanos of Washington, Oregon and California. We learned about the lake that to that point no one had been able to sound far enough to know how deep it was. An ancient volcano, its insides now a deep and dark lake. On the way out of those mountains, my Mom's beautiful new station wagon covered in mud from the slurry slung up from the tires when we came to a place that many years later my Mother finally found out was an old clay pit for the Native Americans of that area. The beautiful grayish clay, was NOT beautiful as it turned into what to me was like a ski track for the car. My Mother was doing her best to keep the car checked by driving with her gears, the brakes could not work in the thick and slick mud. Finally, my Mom ran off the road into a side of the cliff, rather than off the other side of the road and DOWN however many hundreds of feet into the fog and rain. Some people came by and helped her get back on track, and we lived to tell the story of mud skilling in our car.

On a summer road trip, the infamous Oregon and California forest fires started. In the late fifties there were no freeways, few four lane roads, and often nowhere to go except the one road. The main road, with trucks, lumber trucks heading to the mills and other cars was directed to drive all two, or four lanes going south, as the fires were heading south, driven by winds up to fifty and sixty miles per hour. The few gas stations were anxiety ridden as people got gas and quickly back on the road before the fire reached them. In some areas the stations had run out of gas, and some government trucks gave out ten gallons of gas so drivers could get to the next station. One summer, many of the Native sites, and the ghost towns left from the gold rush, that we had stopped and visited on previous trips burned to the ground. We just kept driving. My MOM kept driving. It was so tense, the three of us, all under ten, did not even bother to argue as we usually did on long drives. Like the Alaska road falling into the flooded river, and the dynamited mountain sloughing down on the cars, we just knew, this was a serious and possibly deadly *situation. My Mom always had a big box of food and canteens filled with water, My Grandmother always had her big picnic hamper filled with bread, crackers, cheese in little bottles, jam, peanut butter and fruit to get us through.*

Unlike today, there were NO major stores, NO fast food restaurants. Just a few gas stations, and the government gas trucks, and a scary drive for hundreds of miles. The smoke and ash swirling around ahead of the fire, and especially at night, the constant red/orange light of the fires. The ashes blowing in the winds caused more and more fires to start. The firefighters were doing their best, they did not have water dropping helicopters, or fire retardant dropping planes. Just more and more people, often pulling trailers of stock, trying to outrun the fires. The wild animals found lakes, rivers, and often ran as far as the ocean to stand in the wet sand, the surf pounding around their legs, no fear, no fighting, no eating one another, just waiting for the fire to finish, so they could go back to what was left of their forest homes. Highway 1 was the road along the cliffs and the edge of the beaches, much of it just wild lands, and forests….and people bringing their families and animals to stand in the surf among the wild animals, all turned to watch the fires as they burned down to the sand, and without fuel, burnt out.

Again, we had quite some stories of "what I did on my vacation" when school started up again.

Many students are NOT encouraged to talk about, or write about their life experiences, parents, and teachers, librarians can ask children and teens to write stories. Create books from them, show them how to gather pictures, or make drawings, and create covers and make their own books. Passing these books around the school district, and learning experiences of others helps young people know that THEY are NOT the only ones who have had strange, or horrible experiences. Asking Grandparents and elderly neighbors and relatives as well as parents, helps children and teens learn how to listen to a story, how to write it and retell it, and how to become interested in something more in life.

Another amazing trip we took, my sister and I, my brother going off to Scout camp, was on the magnificent cruises our Grandmother, and her sister-in-law, Lily took after my Mother returned to work and could not take time off the long road trips. These were the luxury liners cruising from Washington State to Alaska. We usually took a train to Washington, and a ferry to Victoria and Vancouver where we stayed at the world famous Victoria Hotel. The Grand Tea at that hotel, each afternoon drew locals, and tourists from around the world visiting the gardens and museums in Victoria and Vancouver. In those days there were somewhat segregated parts of the cities, French, British, and Canadian area. The Native Canadians were not allowed into the cities in those fifties and sixties.

There were parts of town that had Irish, Scottish, and British restaurants and stores. Many of the storefronts made to look like old seventeen or eighteen hundred cities from the old countries. Many street vendors sold flowers, fish and chips wrapped in newspaper with malt vinegars as distinct as the number of vendors.

My sister and I would play "Princess" on the ships, and in the hotel, whether in our kids shorts and shirt waists as my Grandmother called our upscale tee shirts, or dressing in the dresses we had brought to wear to formal restaurants and high teas.

I have never seen any other teas of that quality, and grandness. Great Aunt Lily had been a war bride, brought home by one of my Grandfather's brothers during World War I. She had NOT been a grand lady, she spoke like Eliza in the play "Pygmalion" before she was trained by the Professors to pass as a lady.

The tea desserts and sandwiches, and trays of strawberries, and other fruit bites, as well as trays of many kinds of cheese were set out on huge tables, but, the waiting staff brought you what you asked for. The tea was served in beautiful pots brought to each table and brewed depending on the flavor your table selected.

On the ships, my sister and I would come down the stairs of the grand ballroom, empty during the day, and announce ourselves with our best Beatles accent….and flow down the stairs. We had no idea most girls had not taken ballet and learned early how to flow, not sludge as our ballet teacher called slumping and stumping your feet and holding on to the rail. It would be years before proms or modeling in which we actually had to walk down stairs in long formal dresses, without holding the rails, and flowing, not sludging down, like pigs in satin, as our Russian born, and both Russian and French trained ballet teacher liked to say most women looked coming down stairs in formal affairs.

The ships all sailed just far enough out that we could not see land, and it is a wonderful memory to think of the sea, the view from the decks, and the wonderful formal dinners all the passengers enjoyed. AND the glacier. Once far into the Alaskan waters, the ships moved closer to shore, and after a day or two out of Vancouver or Victoria, we would see glaciers, rising so majestically out of the cold blue seas. Sometimes, since it was a cooling time of year, we would see whales beginning their long trip to the south, to California, Mexico and S. America to the places where they calved and fed before returning to the north the following spring to feed on the varied diets of the different types of whales.

Unless you have seen a whale, with two or three year old calf at her side, blowing water high into the sky, you will not know the breath taking reality of these animals and why it is so important to save them. And to save the ocean for them to play in. For the whales themselves, and for the next generations forever of human children to see and be delighted and awed watching.

Chapter Nine

Ghost Towns, Mother Lode, Snow Cones with real berry flavors, Forest Fires from Washington to the Cajon Pass ……full speed and learning about Nuclear War.

Other kids used to talk about their vacations when school started and we all shared "what I did on my vacation". We lived near Disneyland, Knott's Berry Farm, and at that time Santa Monica Pier and its amusement park and of course Hollywood, the La Brea Tar Pits, and the big Exposition Park natural history museums. and the beaches, skiing, and camping all over Southern California.

I used to feel a little strange, we went mud skiing on mud slides, drove as fast as possible to get away from forest fires, through three states, sat on roads falling into the flooded river in Alaska, waiting to be rescued by the ONE little ferry that could carry four cars, or one truck or bus…..Most of the trucks had to be left in a mud parking lot, the drivers hitching a ride on the busses, or with other drivers.

We did of course go to all the places and eat all the awesome foods, Raspberry pie, the berries were still grown in berry fields around Knott's BERRY farm, the chicken dinners worth the hour drive from Pasadena. Even though my Mom had to do the driving. After I learned to drive, still worth it, and we could bring home a pie, and jam. Except for Mom, we were not sweet eaters, a pie could last for days, and jam for weeks, a tiny dab of it on the awesome multigrain bread my Mom got from the still home delivery Dairy, toasted of course.

There were few freeways at that time. Four lane roads were how we got there. If the traffic was bad, it could take hours to get to the beach, or one of the big parks, or home again. But in those days, there were no drive by shootings, and people played games in the cars, kid games that taught kids to read, about colors, and sizes, as well as shapes. "Who sees a small purple sign that has a W….in it" you could make up anything and the kids would be looking so they could win nickels to spend at the parks, instead of saying over and over "what is the PIN??" or "are we there yet". My Mom used to say, we get there when we get there, anyone who asks are we there yet is going to get

LESS to spend when we get there. We had to do chores, earn our own allowance, and bring some of it to spend, so she meant we were going to get a fine if we bothered her while driving.

It would be years before we overheard her talking to another Mom about their horrible accidents. My Mom had been hit by a car, shoved under a big truck, if she had not been driving an old fashioned car with a huge logo animal on the hood, her car would have slid under the truck, cutting off her head. SHE was a fearful driver, yet she took us all, two little O L D ladies, and three Y O U N G kids on all those road trips. Her friend had been driving slowly down a street, when a kid shot out of house with a long hedge along the driveway. She did not see him behind that hedge, he ran down the hedge, and into the street, right under the wheels of her car and was killed. She drove only when she absolutely had to for her family, and then drove slow, slow, slow.

These ladies wanted it Q U I E T when they drove, it might have been better if either, or both of them had told us what had happened to them. In those days, your Mom said quiet in the car, you knew it meant quiet.

When my older son was born, I found myself shouting at his little toddler self, recognized my Mom, and said that is not going to be me. My Mom had been a teacher, a Sunday School teacher and choir Master at her huge church, she was always calm and strict, but at home she often left out the calm. I went to aa parenting class.

That class taught us that your child needs to understand that you are the pack leader (I would say is the easiest way to explain all their psychiatric blah, blah) or it is anxious and feel unsafe in the world. A child, they explained is not capable of running itself, let alone the family and will develop serious problems if not reined in (my horse word, not their long winded talks). They said every child needs to understand, there is a time and place where people are going to break, that can be sooner, or later, depending on the person, and the circumstances.

Decide what that point is, and WITH your child make some rules that stick. Most parents in those days had a special belt, OR God forbid sent their children out to choose which stick they were going to get whipped with off the nearest tree. A slipper waving in the air, OR I am going to tell your Dad, GO TO YOUR ROOM, all signaled you had just about reached that point and might end up on the front page of the paper as a dead, or missing child.

Many of the kids I knew grew up in the "Wait until your FATHER gets home". I had several friends that without parenting classes, had a Mother who met her husband at the door with a shouted, and often crying list of the sins of the kids that he had to address. Being O L D and having had to deal with working all day, driving home with idiots trying to kill me eon al sides with their bad driving, and coming in the door needing to use the bathroom so badly my eyes were yellow....I now know why those Dads were so mean. Today we attempt to teach Mothers to deal with things immediately, and calmly, and Dads making it clear, YOU deal with YOUR day, I will deal with them when I am dealing with them. For old persons, we might realize that when DAD was watching his games on television.....the kids did NOT run around, screaming and fighting and knocking things down was they did in those old days while Mom was home alone.

For my Mom, she was Mom and Dad most of the time, and though she managed it for her clients and students, often just turned into raging Mom and Dad when she felt like it. To tell the truth, most of us, boomers, new age kids, generation X Y or Z kids.......when we get older, wonder why our parents did not just beat us to death. One woman said, when asked if she had kids, said yes, ONE, and that is two too many. Most parents today know what that means. What if you had six, or ten, or twelve. No wonder families had two old Aunties and a housekeeper and a nanny living there, just homeless family members they gave a room in exchange for helping them not kill the kids.

Yet, we all remember those packed holiday dinners, planks on saw horses if need be, kids at little tables around the house with pillows to sit on around the coffee table. Grandparents, parents remembering old holidays. Not like to many families today, feeling forced to dress up and go to a house, or hotel and be with people they do not like and would rather stay home and eat in their pajamas.

Big bowls of olives, with kids under the table, reaching up and grabbing a few, sticking them on their fingers, then eating them off. Big plates of that old white bread you could nibble the crust off, and then crush into a small hard ball and eat like a golf ball. Who knew what kids had passed that right of passage along, or when you were too old to sit under the table eating olives and bread golf balls?

We, as kids seem to do, feel embarrassed that few just did not have the same old vacations as everyone else. Of course, my Mom worked with families that had NO vacations. A vacation to them was to go to the laundromat, seriously, so they did not have to carry buckets of water to the backyard, fill a big silver tub with water, and one with detergent water and wash the clothes for vacation. Maybe they got to go to the movies and get one popcorn to share for the whole family. BUT did we care? No. Today, looking back we had amazing adventures, met people and ate foods, and did things no one else GOT to do.

Including going to the laundry with a bunch of kids because their Mom was sick, our Mom had once been their social worker, was now their friend…..and she had a car, so those kids did not have to carry pillow cases full of dirty clothes to the Laundromat and clean clothes back home. We of course "got" to help them with the laundry. Our Mom worked, had a laundry room at the house, and a full time housekeeper after I was 12. She felt the three of us could get along without her as she returned to work as a Deputy of Adoptions and Foster Care. It was a good experience for us to go "play" with kids who played by taking many loads of laundry to the laundromat instead of having to wash it in a tub in the yard, or in the bathtub and hang it on the fence and shrubs. My Mom would load up all the laundry and drop all of us kids at the laundromat, and sit on a chair and do her paperwork while we helped those kids do that laundry.

Chapter Ten

Dining in OLD Chinatown, Los Angeles, and San Francisco

My Mother had grown up in Pasadena, with a Great Aunt who was a world class scientist at both Cal Tech (a block from the house) and at Cornell, across the country. My Grandparents were a great mixture of different groups that had come to America to escape the lack of freedom and dreams caused by the euro monarchs and despots. They had many religions between their family members, and knew many people of all cultures, religions and financial backgrounds.

My Mom grew up going to Christmas at her own home with people of all different religions invited over for the holiday. The Thanksgivings of those years at their home were big multi-cultural events. All those that had survived wars, pogroms and genocides had special thanks at being in America and came with a variety of foods to share.

At the Rez, three women were the ones who survived the genocide in Northern California during and following the "gold rush". The rules against incest caused them, and their first daughters and nieces to marry outside our nations ..... the young men, who had been babies and taken with the women, disabled and elders to escape the bounty hunters also due to incest rules, had to marry outside our own culture. Again, a large quantity of races, cultures and religions was the result.

We had no idea that we grew up in a small group of Americans, and humans, who just liked other people and shared all their culture, history and love with one another.

My Mother worked in many counties while going to school, and getting her licenses and teaching credential. She loved the people she worked with, did NOT see them as less than she, just people who needed a hand up to make it through the real. world and help their children have better lives.

My Grandmother and Mother had both been teachers, they taught. While working at the ER, where sooner or later everyone in town comes for one reason or another, I met many older women who told me awesome stories of how my Grandmother had taught them piano, and then to be piano teachers, just to share the music and the love of playing piano. She taught them art, and cooking as she learned it herself. THEY taught her how to keep her house and garden. She had grown up with maids, housekeepers, nanny and governess. Landscapers, and chef. She would laugh and say my Grandfather had married a woman who knew it all, was Dean of a college, but did not know how to boil water for an egg, or how to make coffee properly.

From a wealthy family himself, before he took off to the wild west to become a miner, and real estate dabbler, He bought much of what today is Laguna, Palm Desert, La Quinta and Balboa as investments, but after he passed her lawyer tricked her into turning it into cash for her retirement. Property she sold for ten times what my Grandfather paid for it is now as much as millions of times what he paid for it. Just one lot in La Quinta, a few years after she had sold it to the lawyer, sold for more than he had paid for all the real estate he had bought, including the two houses he had put on the Pasadena lots. My Grandfather too, had had to learn to make coffee over a fire, became a stone mason, did construction and finally settled down as a beat cop, and eventually became a homicide detective in Pasadena Police Department.

Between them they knew and loved everyone. The statement by Will Rogers, "I never met a man I didn't like" was surely true for my Grandparents. And I am sure there was not ever a person that didn't love them. My Grandfather would give advice to people he arrested, and tell them, no matter if they spent time in prison, find a better way and come out to help their children and families. It was not uncommon for a nicely dressed person to come and thank him for believing in them at a time they did not believe in themselves and helping them find faith in God, and in themselves to do better for themselves and their families.

Every holiday, whether their religion or not, they received cards, presents, flowers, and baskets of fruit, wine, cheese and thanks from people who believed they had changed their lives. I did not know as a child what rare people these were, most of their relatives were the same.

On the other side of my family, I saw the racism, the pain, the unequal treatment. My Mom was there for several years, and the years she took us to visit our relatives and learn about our culture and family she always helped the family overcome and survive that racism and inequality. She helped people step out, get an education, use their VA benefits to buy homes, ranches and get a higher education. She created a sense of self worth that had been missing before she came. I do not think we valued this as children, but as adults realize it is why our Rez has a better understanding and feeling of worth for our ancestors and traditions than many others.

These childhood experiences and respect for everyone led us to meet a lot of people our parents, and Grandparents had known of all different cultures, races, religions AND got us invited to local events or traditional events non-members of those cultures, religions or races rarely had the opportunity to attend, as family, not weird tourists.

My Mother had worked in both San Francisco and Los Angeles in child services. She therefore had many friends in the Chinatown's of both big cities. We would go to dinner at restaurants with her friends that only the Chinese and their guests knew how to find. How different from the local "chinese" delivery restaurants most people knew at that time.

We would go and see the elders teaching the young people the dances, and how to repair and build new dragons for the New Year ceremony and parade. All the children laughing and yet being very respectful when being taught. AND those kids cleaned everything up when asked, whether it was their mess or not. I noticed early that there were NO janitors forced to clean up after people too lazy to clean up after themselves. OR to clean up messes left by people who did not care they were making someone's job harder. Little old ladies and little old men often came with their own brooms, and swept, having a child with them to bend down with the dust pan and help get all the mess into the waste bins. I noticed when we left, the area was as clean, or cleaner, then when the event started.

Chapter Eleven

BRINGING IN THE COWS TO MILK, AND ELECTRIC CATTLE FENCING

When we were in our teens, my Dad remarried (another time, he did not believe in living with anyone without being married) and we would go for his custody months over the summer.

We would visit his in-laws home, which was a sizable dairy farm. Other relatives had built homes on or near the main house and barns. What a change for city kids. We did of course know that eggs came from chickens, ours were delivered with the milk from the van that still delivered milk, bread, eggs, butter, and other daily products three days a week.

The first time we visited the dairy, we were told to go get the cows for milking. There were long lanes, and gates to open or close so the cows did not use the same pasture every day, it gave the grass time to recover. So those cows did not live in mud, and were not covered with mud. They were kept clean, and every day when they came in to be milked were washed and groomed as well.

My Grandmother had what she pointed out to us was the Biblical rule that if a human used an animal for work, that animal deserved life care. She had her cows keep their calves, she said, if I cannot afford two or three extra cows so the cows and calves are treated humanely, I should get out of this business. God came first to her. AND God created those animals and gave us a duty to care for them.

Of course, we did not know that on our first day, they said bring in the cows. We opened the gate, and most of the cows just headed down the lane to the barn. We would learn later that every cow kept her calves for life. The steers were sterilized in their first year, but just remained with the rest of the herd. We did not know…..so we spent a long time chasing those steers in to the barn, where we got a good laughing at from the barn hands milking the cows. The steers got a little treat and sent back to the field. In winter the cows had barns, in summer they spent the nights out with trees and little sheds to cover them if needed. The cows would get their grain, cleaned, checked for injuries, and milked, then sent back to the field.

The chickens were in hundreds, lived in the fields, and the barns, they each found their own tree or place in the barn to roost at night, but otherwise were on their own. My Grandmother fed them in large hen feeders, and smaller chick feeders. NO ONE was allowed to butcher those chickens except her. She had her favorites, and of course did NOT want some dummy to kill her laying hens. It was again, a shock, yet became an important part of life to see how fast and humanely she dispatched the chickens, ducks, or geese that would end up a meal, or sold to someone to help pay for the feed for the rest of the flocks.

The lanes were just lanes, no electric wires, but some of the fields were bordered on at least once side by highway, road, or driveway. Those fences had electric wires. Of course the kind farm kids, and workers did NOT tell us WHY the cows need only one run in with those wires and they stay away. We were running through the fields one day, and NONE of us has ever forgotten what just one touch of those wires feels like, and it has been a good fifty years.

Chapter Twelve

Closing:

The last three or four books in our selection are in response to a request that we give free help to the children and teens in the world concentration camps for children and teens. We, as humans, have the opportunity to look at our Principles and to design better global support for families and children.

This particular book is for children; to utilize storytelling as a means to attempt to reach deep into the broken hearts and broken souls of children and teens, to help them heal themselves and each other before throwing away their own lives in bitterness, anger, hate, angst and self-pity. We are including here a teen designed program from the late 1980's which in their final survey they said they needed earlier, so we said, then help kids design and implement one. KJr.

Our youngest member was two, involved in a family divorce, our oldest, 18 coming with his disabled brother during his summer vacation before leaving for college.

The basic Rights of a CHILD said the kids:

The right to be wanted
The right to belong
The right to harmonious surroundings
The right to a spiritual and moral upbringing
The right to GOOD nutrition
The right to GOOD medical care
The right to clothes that are clean and appropriate
The right to personal space

The right to personal safety

The right to make a mistake

The right to an education that will lead to personal fulfillment and employment and an opportunity to pursue it peacefully and at one's own pace

The right to love and be loved without outside interference as long as no one is harmed by the relationship (molesting juveniles is NOT about love)

The programs are run by KIDS, never an adult professional of any kind. A teacher, probation officer, pastor may "oversee" the programs, but is NOT to interfere as long as the program is being adhered to without injury or bullying by any member of the group.

In the workbooks that go with these programs, the youth and children work within each one-hour meeting to help the others go over these Twelve Rights. The quasi Twelve Steps which are included in our training manual as well.

The basic Rights of a CHILD said the kids: In our workbooks, each child or teen is given a blank sheet spiral notebook to work in and is expected to do the exercises and share their insights to help others heal.

The right to be wanted- Children of the richest most powerful parents often realize their father did NOT want them, and their mother had them to get money and position from the father, and/or a picture person for the albums and videos of family events. The children realize in the groups that there is NO child who is always wanted. A child wanted and loved by parents may be sent to a school, or orphan home and /or refugee camp with people who survived when their own parents and family did not. We ask the children to work on drawing themselves and how they feel. This work page was so successful that parents, teachers, probation officers and even judges did this work and healed their own inner child. Ps 227:10, no matter what religions a person is part of, says that the Creator of ALL never forsakes us, if every other human, even our birth parents, have for some reason left our lives, our Creator is still there, and will never forsake us.

It is our position that like breath God is more than likely not concerned with what puny human definitions and rules are put out as "the truth", it does not matter what word in any language is breath, without it you will not live. Without a trust and faith in our Creator, we are not going to survive. Even atheists. Ps 27:10 does NOT say we have to believe it says the universal entity will not forsake us.

The right to belong: The United Nations says as part of its ten rights and responsibilities for every human on earth, is to belong somewhere. We have failed as humans to take responsibility to see that this right is there for every single human on earth. The children talk about this in their own lives, and in the lives of humans worldwide. What is this right, and what are the responsibilities that go with that right.

The right to harmonious surroundings These children, most of them in divorces, in orphanages, from refugee camps saw the right that every child should have harmonious surroundings. THIS DOES NOT MEAN one cultures idea of what that is……it does mean no poverty. Many ancient cultures have had traditions that made sure every child had this right along with the right to a place to belong. The stories were often made up that the Native Americans kidnapped "beautiful" children from the white genocidal intruders. In fact, the wagon trains, and families who left on foot to go to the west often were killed by floods, heat, no water, running out of food, and disease. Native people had a tradition that they could not leave a child alone, so when they came upon these sad scenes, they took the children to the long houses where children were raised and raised them. Children of all races and cultures looked at this right, at the history of the world, and how it fit into their own lives. Orphanages, or bad foster homes were NOT harmonious surroundings. Every city that has a single foster child needs to have mentor families and persons who HELP the family raising the foster child. This worked in Los Angeles for several years, for children, disabled, and elderly when County Supervisor Baxter Ward proposed a volunteer run program that gave every single child, disabled and elderly person a mentor to watch out and care for them. This was about HELPING not snitching or tattle tales or punishment ….it was about seeing those needing help, got care, and love.

The right to a spiritual and moral upbringing This is NOT about religion. It is NOT about some panel making up what is right or wrong, good or bad. It is about helping young people, first by being good role models, to grow up to be people who love themselves, and love others in the same manner......to teach children and teens that in America laws are made by people who look and see what is best for everyone and is administrated by a system of justice (now that you have all stopped choking while rolling on the ground laughing yourselves sick, think about how amazing it would be if we all lived to be our best and help others be their best instead of trying to get something over on everyone before they get something over on us). Courts are supposed to be there to give ALL people EQUAL justice, so they do not go out breaking people's knees or worse to get justice. In America, lawyers used to go to school for two years, take a test, and go work in a law office or judges court to learn to make our laws JUST. Today, we are figuratively seeing a lot more broken knees by people who do not get justice in the courts. Whether tiny, or 18, kids need to understand our principles and why we ALL need to work to make them work.

The right to GOOD nutrition: Whether in your own family, or in foster care, or in those big concentration camps of children America has put together, children deserve GOOD nutrition. NOT the cheapest, most gluey, worst mess someone can sell to the government or the food banks overpriced and who cares?

Children need to know, a bowl of cereal, even sugar coated cereal, with either milk, or a good calcium containing milk replacement and a piece of fruit, IF the cereal is NOT sugar coated, is OK for a child or teen. A piece of high grain bread, a piece of cheese, or peanut butter or other nut spread, fine. But not with soda or sugar filled drink instead of the milk or milk substitute.

Children can have a free choice vegetable, fruit and bread with peanut butter or other nut spread in the snack area for recesses and lunch to keep them with positive nutrition. Crackers, juice, (NOT sugar mix, but real juice) in SMALL cups so they do not waste is fine for snacks. BUT children need a school nurse to help them each learn their own history and what or what they need to avoid. A child that comes to pre-school fat needs to see a doctor, and the school nurse needs to help that child and others, to figure out their own GOOD nutrition for THAT child, not their eighteen year old athlete brother or sister.

The right to GOOD medical care children deserve good medical care. SCHOOL NURSES. When we were kids every school had a school nurse. The school nurse had volunteer Mothers, and a list of doctors that could see kids in emergency on specific days, IF the child did not have a regular pediatrician to send the child to. Vaccines were just beginning, also antibiotics were not well known, but a pediatrician visit included shots, vaccines, and pills as needed, NO prescriptions or waits at pharmacies with sick kids….Nutrition, dental check-ups, cleanings, volunteer parents with the huge dental dinosaur puppets and huge toothbrushes and huge dental floss to show kids how to take care of their teeth, as well as personalized calendars for the children to take home, and stickers for each morning and evening all were taught to every child, local dentists usually donated cases of toothbrushes and toothpaste right for each age of child as well as discounts for families that needed them on x-ray and simple fillings. We can do that again. Think of all the jobs, and the cost would be less than welfare, food cards, and medical care for the workers. Not just one country, every country within ninety days. WOW.

The right to clothes that are clean and appropriate Again, the school nurse. These nurses used to watch the children and if they did not have good, clean clothing, the nurse talked to the parents (at that time many were single parent mothers after the war, their spouse had died, or had what today we call PTSD, and had left the family, or was at home not able to help with financial care of the children. Volunteer Mothers would bring in clothing, take it home as needed and wash, and iron it as needed. Parents asked their churches and community groups to donate clothing that was most often needed. These nurses knew how to make sure kids were taken care of without embarrassment or bullying by other children. Especially in the area we grew up in, the nurses would call in parents and all talk about bullying when any child was bullied for their clothing, or hygiene. Once a child was brought into the ER where I worked, he was maybe 14, and thee doctor said, please, take him upstairs and have him take a shower, I can't work on him in this condition. I called up to one of the pediatric units, and met a nurse who showed the teen where to take a shower, I waited, and waited….. it was obvious he was enjoying that shower, and taking a LONG time taking it. When we went back down to the ER, I asked him, if you love showers so much, how come you don't take them at home, he said, honestly "no water". Nurses used to make sure the MAYOR knew about families without utilizes and in a day or two a social working came out and set out a plan to get the utilities back on, and to help the parents pay their utilities on time. Sometimes this means financial counseling, sometimes it means help with school and jobs.

The right to personal space Every child deserve personal space. Whether a shoebox or knapsack of homework tools, in a corner, or a room to study in, or just an hour or two in a crowded place, every child deserves personal space…

The right to personal safety children and teens need to learn to feel safe, in order to allow others to feel safe around them. Again, the school nurse is the one who used to watch the children and was the one who often talked to the Principal about a child that was being bullied at school, or possibly being abused at home. Today all fire stations are supposed to be safe places for children and teens to go and ask for help with abuse or bullying that makes them unsafe. It is also up to the Mayor, and all the adults in the community to make sure all children are SAFE. Working with Racial Tension and Gang Abatement projects the children, and teens told us they wanted safe places to live. There is NO excuse for children, teens, disabled and/or seniors to be unsafe, whether from crime, or war….or financial bullying. We, as adults need to resolve these issues.

The right to make a mistake. Everyone deserves the right to make mistakes, especially children and teens. Again that school nurse is the one who often hears from teachers, or other students that children and teens are being abused for not being the "perfect" student, athlete, everything their parents wanted to be, but were not. In one program we had to tell the parents who came to "sideline coach" their children to either NOT come, to sit in their cars, or to pay extra for materials and do the activities themselves. Most of the parents enjoyed the activities, but often did not do as well as their children and teens. So much for their sides line expertise. More than one child or teen has thanked us for straight forward telling their parents or grandparents that if THEY wanted to go to college, or be whatever old dream of their own they were trying to foist on to their family child or teen, they needed to go and find out how to get there themselves, not steal their child's childhood and own dreams. Sometimes we were not popular for doing this, but kids had told us of children and teens being beaten up behind the gym for not being the BEST player of the day, or in the car being punched and screamed at for a paper that was not A, A, A, A. We stepped in and talked to the police child protection services and made sure those children and teens were protected. One of the worst excuses is that "our family is not from this country", well, we said, "in this country, it is a crime, maybe even a felony to beat and abuse your children and teens".

The right to an education that will lead to personal fulfillment and employment and an opportunity to pursue it peacefully and at one's own pace. Every child has the right to an education that is more than just an enforced prison filled with gangs, violence and non-learning. While teaching at some of the most prestigious pre-schools and kindergartens and then comparing them to public schools I volunteered in I was shocked. Then I began to meet teachers and psychiatrists who were learning specialists who claimed there was a movement to make sure children did NOT learn to meet their dreams. To be equipped to take and pass tests for licensing that would allow them to rise in their fields of work. This, upon research is exactly what the Founders of America did NOT want, that is why the Constitution says explicitly that NO ONE can CREATE and Elite. That five percent academic testing model does exactly that. Many professionals have complained that testing to get into programs is unrelated to the real work of the field, but contains questions only really rich kids would know the answers to, OR kids who have taken expensive train to the test classes. That is not OK. Children should not be expected in tenth grade to learn all that others have learned over sixteen years in order to pass the tests needed to get into elite education programs where those who will hold the licenses to get paid for all jobs, get the education while those who DO the jobs do not.

The right to love and be loved without outside interference as long as no one is harmed by the relationship (molesting juveniles is NOT about love). Children have a right to be loved. This means that their parents need to NOT just arrogantly be removed from their lives by social workers or courts that think THEY know better in foster group "care" how to care for those children. It does NOT mean that children have to grow up without food, safety, clothing, education, healthcare because society does not help them have those rights, or forces love away to get the other rights. LOVE also means that when they are old enough, children and teens have a right to love those they choose. BUT we all, humans need to stop thinking it is OK for children or young teens to make a decision of who they are because of societal mores and pressures. If a kid wants to wear a football uniform to school because SHE likes it, let her. If a kid wants to wear a prom dress to school everyday, because HE loves it, let him….BUT kids need to know that sex is real, and it can create babies that deserve ALL these rights and incurs huge responsibilities. Kids have a right to know that adults that urge them into, or force them to have sex are molesters, and NOT out for their best interest…….this is a sensitive area, but people deserve to love and be loved by someone who LOVES them and who they LOVE. This needs a lot of discussion by the kids to figure it out, without fear, or pressure, from either side of the issues.

Other books in our programs:

Other Books by Author and team

Closing:

All of our group of books, and workbooks contain some work pages, and/or suggestions for the reader, and those teaching these books to make notes, to go to computer, and libraries and ask others for information to help these projects work their best.

To utilize these to their fullest, make sure YOU model the increased thoughts and availability of more knowledge to anyone you share these books and workbooks with in classes, or community groups.

Magazines are, as noted in most of the books, a wonderful place to look for and find ongoing research and information. Online search engines often bring up new research in the areas, and newly published material.

We all have examples of how we learned and who it was that taught us.

One of the strangest lessons I have learned was walking to a shoot in downtown Los Angeles. The person who kindly told me to park my truck in Pasadena, and take the train had been unaware that the weekend busses did NOT run early in the morning when the crews had to be in to set up. That person, being just a participant, was going much later in the day, taking a taxi, and had no idea how often crews do NOT carry purses with credit cards, large amounts of cash, and have nowhere to carry those items, because the crew works hard, and fast during a set up and tear down and after the shoot are TIRED and not looking to have to find items that have been left around, or stolen.

As I walked, I had to travel through an area of Los Angeles that had become truly run down and many homeless were encamped about and sleeping on the sidewalks and in alleys. I saw a man, that having worked in an ER for many years I realized was DEAD. I used to have thoughts about people who did not notice people needing help, I thought, this poor man, this is probably the most peace he has had in a long time. I prayed for him and went off to my unwanted walk across town. As I walked, I thought about myself, was I just heartless, or was I truly thinking this was the only moment of peace this man had had for a long time and just leaving him to it. What good were upset neighbors, and police, fire trucks and ambulances going to do. He was calmly, eyes open, staring out at a world that had failed him while alive, why rush to disturb him now that nothing could be done.

I did make sure he was DEAD. He was, quite cold rigid.

I learned that day that it is best to do what a person needs, NOT what we need.

Learning is about introspection and grounding of material. Passing little tests on short term memory skills and not knowing what it all means is NOT education, or teaching.

As a high school student, in accelerated Math and Science programs, in which I received 4.0 grades consistently, I walked across a field, diagonally, and suddenly all that math and science made sense, it was not just exercises on paper I could throw answers back on paper, but I realized had NO clue as to what it all really meant.

OTHER BOOKS
by this author, and team

Most, if not all, of these books are written at a fourth grade level. First, the author is severely brain damaged from a high fever disease caused by a sample that came in the mail, without a warning that it had killed during test marketing. During the law suit, it was discovered that the corporation had known prior to mailing out ten million samples, WITHOUT warnings of disease and known deaths, and then NOT telling anyone after a large number of deaths around the world started. Second, the target audience is high risk youth, and young veterans, most with a poor education before signing into, or being drafted into the military as a hope Many of our veterans are Vietnam or WWII era.

Maybe those recruiting promises would come true. They would be trained, educated, and given chance for a home, and to protect our country and its principles. Watch the movies Platoon, and Born on the Fourth of July as well as the Oliver Stone series on history to find out how these dreams were meet.

DO NOT bother to write and tell us of grammar or spelling errors. We often wrote these books and workbooks fast for copyrights. We had learned our lessons about giving our material away when one huge charity asked us for our material, promising a grant, Instead, we heard a couple of years later they had built their own VERY similar project, except theirs charged for services, ours were FREE, and theirs was just for a small group, ours was training veterans and others to spread the programs as fast as they could.. They got a Nobel Peace prize. We keep saying we are not bitter, we keep saying we did not do our work to get awards, or thousands of dollars of grants….but, it hurts. Especially when lied to and that group STILL sends people to US for help when they cannot meet the needs, or the veterans and family cannot afford their "charitable" services. One other group had the nerve to send us a Cease and Desist using our own name. We said go ahead and sue, we have proof of legal use of this name for decades. That man had the conscience to apologize, his program was not even FOR veterans or first responders, or their families, nor high risk kids. But we learned. Sometimes life is very unfair.

We got sued again later for the same issue. We settled out of Court as our programs were just restarting and one of the veterans said, let's just change that part of the name and keep on training veterans to run their own programs. Smart young man.

Book List:

DRAGON KITES and other stories:

The Grandparents Story list will add 12 new titles this year. We encourage every family to write their own historic stories. That strange old Aunt who when you listen to her stories left a rich and well regulated life in the Eastern New York coastal fashionable families to learn Telegraph messaging and go out to the old west to LIVE her life. That old Grandfather or Grandmother who was sent by family in other countries torn by war to pick up those "dollars in the streets" as noted in the book of that title.

Books in publication, or out by summer 2021

Carousel Horse: A Children's book about equine therapy and what schools MIGHT be and are in special private programs.

Carousel Horse: A smaller version of the original Carousel Horse, both contain the workbooks and the screenplays used for on-site stable programs as well as lock down programs where the children and teens are not able to go out to the stables.

Spirit Horse II: This is the work book for training veterans and others interested in starting their own Equine Therapy based programs. To be used as primary education sites, or for supplementing public or private school programs. One major goal of this book is to copyright our founding material, as we gave it away freely to those who said they wanted to help us get grants. They did not. Instead they built their own programs, with grant money, and with donations in small, beautiful stables and won....a Nobel Peace Prize for programs we invented. We learned our lessons, although we do not do our work for awards, or grants, we DO not like to be ripped off, so now we copyright.

Reassessing and Restructuring Public Agencies; This book is an over view of our government systems and how they were expected to be utilized for public betterment. This is a Fourth Grade level condemnation of a PhD dissertation that was not accepted be because the mentor thought it was "against government".. The first paragraph noted that a request had been made, and referrals given by the then White House.

Reassessing and Restructuring Public Agencies; TWO. This book is a suggestive and creative work to give THE PEOPLE the idea of taking back their government and making the money spent and the agencies running SERVE the PEOPLE; not politicians. This is NOT against government, it is about the DUTY of the PEOPLE to oversee and control government before it overcomes us.

Could This Be Magic? A Very Short Book. This is a very short book of pictures and the author's personal experiences as the Hall of Fame band VAN HALEN practiced in her garage. The pictures are taken by the author, and her then five year old son. People wanted copies of the pictures, and permission was given to publish them to raise money for treatment and long term Veteran homes.

Carousel TWO: Equine therapy for Veterans. publication pending 2021

Carousel THREE: Still Spinning: Special Equine therapy for women veterans and single mothers. This book includes TWELVE STEPS BACK FROM BETRAYAL for soldiers who have been sexually assaulted in the active duty military and help from each other to heal, no matter how horrible the situation. publication pending 2021

LEGAL ETHICS: AN OXYMORON. A book to give to lawyers and judges you feel have not gotten the justice of American Constitution based law (Politicians are great persons to gift with this book). Publication late 2021

PARENTS CAN LIVE and raise great kids.

Included in this book are excerpts from our workbooks from KIDS ANONYMOUS and KIDS JR, and A PARENTS PLAIN RAP (to teach sexuality and relationships to their children. This program came from a copyrighted project thirty years ago, which has been networked into our other programs. This is our training work book. We asked AA what we had to do to become a real Twelve Step program as this is considered a quasi twelve step program children and teens can use to heal BEFORE becoming involved in drugs, sexual addiction, sexual trafficking and relationship woes, as well as unwanted, neglected and abused or having children murdered by parents not able to deal with the reality of parenting. Many of our original students were children of abuse and neglect, no matter how wealthy. Often the neglect was by society itself when children lost parents to illness, accidents or addiction. We were told, send us a copy and make sure you call it quasi. The Teens in the first programs when surveyed for the outcome research reports said, WE NEEDED THIS EARLIER. SO they helped younger children invent KIDS JR. Will be republished in 2021 as a documentary of the work and success of these projects.

Addicted To Dick. This is a quasi Twelve Step program for women in domestic violence programs mandated by Courts due to repeated incidents and danger, or actual injury or death of their children.

Addicted to Dick 2018. This book is a specially requested workbook for women in custody, or out on probation for abuse to their children, either by themselves or their sexual partners or spouses. The estimated national number for children at risk at the time of request was three million across the nation. During Covid it is estimated that number has risen. Homelessness and undocumented families that are unlikely to be reported or found are creating discussion of a much larger number of children maimed or killed in these domestic violence crimes. THE most important point in this book is to force every local school district to train teachers, and all staff to recognize children at risk, and to report their family for HELP, not punishment. The second most important part is to teach every child on American soil to know to ask for help, no matter that parents, or other relatives or known adults, or unknown adults have threatened to kill them for "telling". Most, if not all paramedics, emergency rooms, and police and fire stations are trained to protect the children and teens, and get help for the family.. PUNISHMENT is not the goal, eliminating childhood abuse and injury or death at the hands of family is the goal of all these projects. In some areas JUDGES of child and family courts were taking training and teaching programs themselves to HELP. FREE..

Addicted to Locker Room BS. This book is about MEN who are addicted to the lies told in locker rooms and bars. During volunteer work at just one of several huge juvenile lock downs, where juveniles who have been convicted as adults, but are waiting for their 18th birthday to be sent to adult prisons, we noticed that the young boys and teens had "big" ideas of themselves, learned in locker rooms and back alleys. Hundreds of these young boys would march, monotonously around the enclosures, their lives over. often facing long term adult prison sentences.

The girls, we noticed that the girls, for the most part were smart, had done well in school, then "something" happened. During the years involved in this volunteer work I saw only ONE young girl who was so mentally ill I felt she was not reachable, and should be in a locked down mental health facility for help; if at all possible, and if teachers, and others had been properly trained, helped BEFORE she gotten to that place, lost in the horror and broken of her childhood and early teen years.

We noticed that many of the young women in non-military sexual assault healing programs were "betrayed" in many ways, by step fathers, boyfriends, even fathers, and mothers by either molestation by family members, or allowing family members or friends of parents to molest these young women, often as small children. We asked military sexually assaulted young women to begin to volunteer to help in the programs to heal the young girls and teens, it helped heal them all.

There was NOTHING for the boys that even began to reach them until our research began on the locker room BS theory of life destruction and possible salvaging by the boys themselves, and men in prisons who helped put together something they thought they MIGHT have heard before they ended up in prison.

Americans CAN Live Happily Ever After. Parents edition One.
Americans CAN Live Happily Ever After. Children's edition Two.

Americans CAN Live Happily Ever After. Three. After Covid. This book includes "Welcome to America" a requested consult workbook for children and youth finding themselves in cages, auditoriums on cots, or in foster group homes or foster care of relatives or non-relatives with NO guidelines for their particular issues. WE ASKED the kids, and they helped us write this fourth grade level workbook portion of this book to help one another and each other. Written in a hurry! We were asked to use our expertise in other youth programs, and our years of experience teaching and working in high risk youth programs to find something to help.

REZ CHEESE Written by a Native American /WASP mix woman. Using food, and thoughts on not getting THE DIABETES, stories are included of a childhood between two worlds.

REZ CHEESE TWO A continuation of the stress on THE DIABETES needing treatment and health care from birth as well as recipes, and stories from Native America, including thoughts on asking youth to help stop the overwhelming numbers of suicide by our people.

BIG LIZ: LEADER OF THE GANG Stories of unique Racial Tension and Gang Abatement projects created when gangs and racial problems began to make schools unsafe for our children.

DOLLARS IN THE STREETS, ghost edited for author Lydia Caceras, the first woman horse trainer at Belmont Park.

95 YEARS of TEACHING:
A book on teaching, as opposed to kid flipping
Two teachers who have created and implemented systems for private and public education a combined 95 plus years of teaching talk about experiences and realities and how parents can get involved in education for their children. Included are excerpts from our KIDS ANONYMOUS and KIDS JR workbooks of over 30 years of free youth programs.

A HORSE IS NOT A BICYCLE. A book about pet ownership and how to prepare your children for responsible pet ownership and along the way to be responsible parents. NO ONE needs to own a pet, or have a child, but if they make that choice, the animal, or child deserves a solid, caring forever home.

OLD MAN THINGS and MARE'S TALES. this is a fun book about old horse trainers I met along the way. My husband used to call the old man stories "old man things", which are those enchanting and often very effective methods of horse, pet, and even child rearing. I always said I brought up my children and my students the same as I had trained horses and dogs……I meant that horses and dogs had taught me a lot of sensible, humane ways to bring up an individual, caring, and dream realizing adult who was HAPPY and loved.

STOP TALKING, DO IT

ALL of us have dreams, intentions, make promises. This book is a workbook from one of our programs to help a person make their dreams come true, to build their intentions into goals, and realities, and to keep their promises. One story from this book, that inspired the concept is a high school kid, now in his sixties, that was in a special ed program for drug abuse and not doing well in school. When asked, he said his problem was that his parents would not allow him to buy a motorcycle. He admitted that he did not have money to buy one, insure one, take proper driver's education and licensing examinations to own one, even though he had a job. He was asked to figure out how much money he was spending on drugs. Wasting his own money, stealing from his parents and other relatives, and then to figure out, if he saved his own money, did some side jobs for neighbors and family until he was 18, he COULD afford the motorcycle and all it required to legally own one. In fact, he did all, but decided to spend the money on college instead of the motorcycle when he graduated from high school. His priorities had changed as he learned about responsible motorcycle ownership and risk doing the assignments needed for his special ed program. He also gave up drugs, since his stated reason was he could not have a motorcycle, and that was no longer true, he COULD have a motorcycle, just had to buy it himself, not just expect his parents to give it to him.

Printed in the United States
by Baker & Taylor Publisher Services